THE Capybara CUTIE CLUB

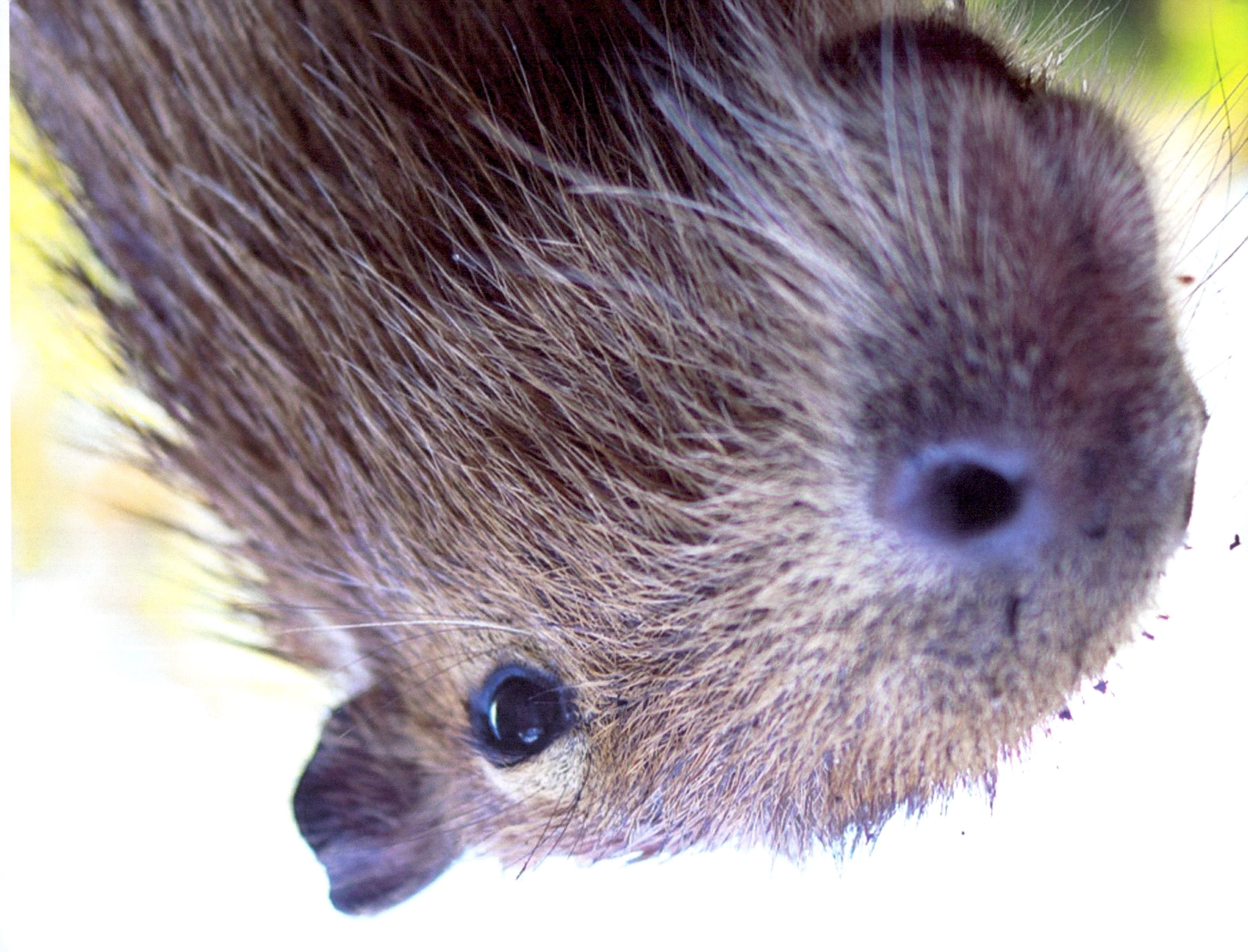

JANUARY 2025

SUNDAY	MONDAY	TUESDAY	WEDNESDAY	THURSDAY	FRIDAY	SATURDAY
29	30	31	1	2	3	4
5	6	7	8	9	10	11
12	13	14	15	16	17	18
19	20	21	22	23	24	25
26	27	28	29	30	31	1

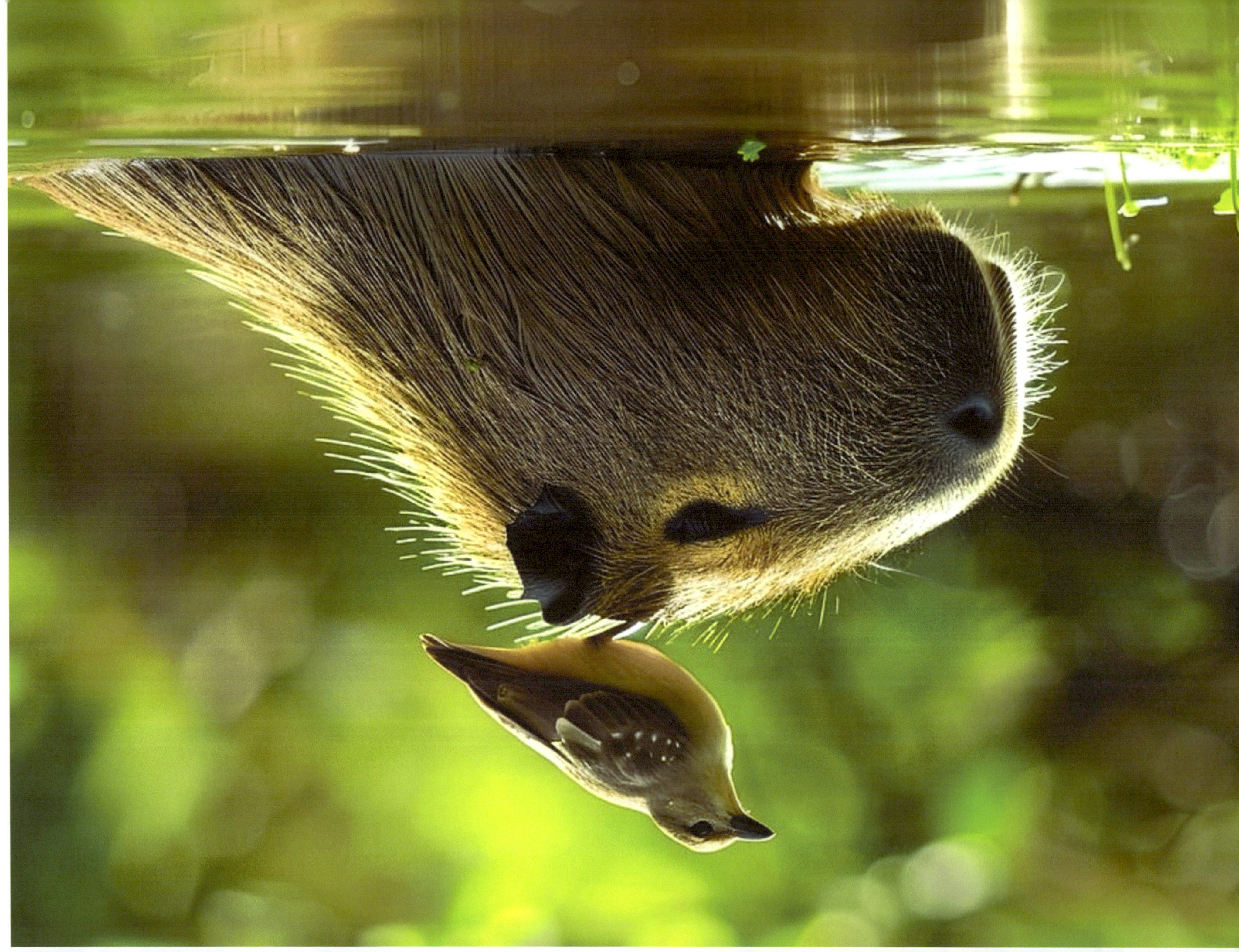

FEBRUARY 2025

SUNDAY	MONDAY	TUESDAY	WEDNESDAY	THURSDAY	FRIDAY	SATURDAY
26	27	28	29	30	31	1
2	3	4	5	6	7	8
9	10	11	12	13	14	15
16	17	18	19	20	21	22
23	24	25	26	27	28	1

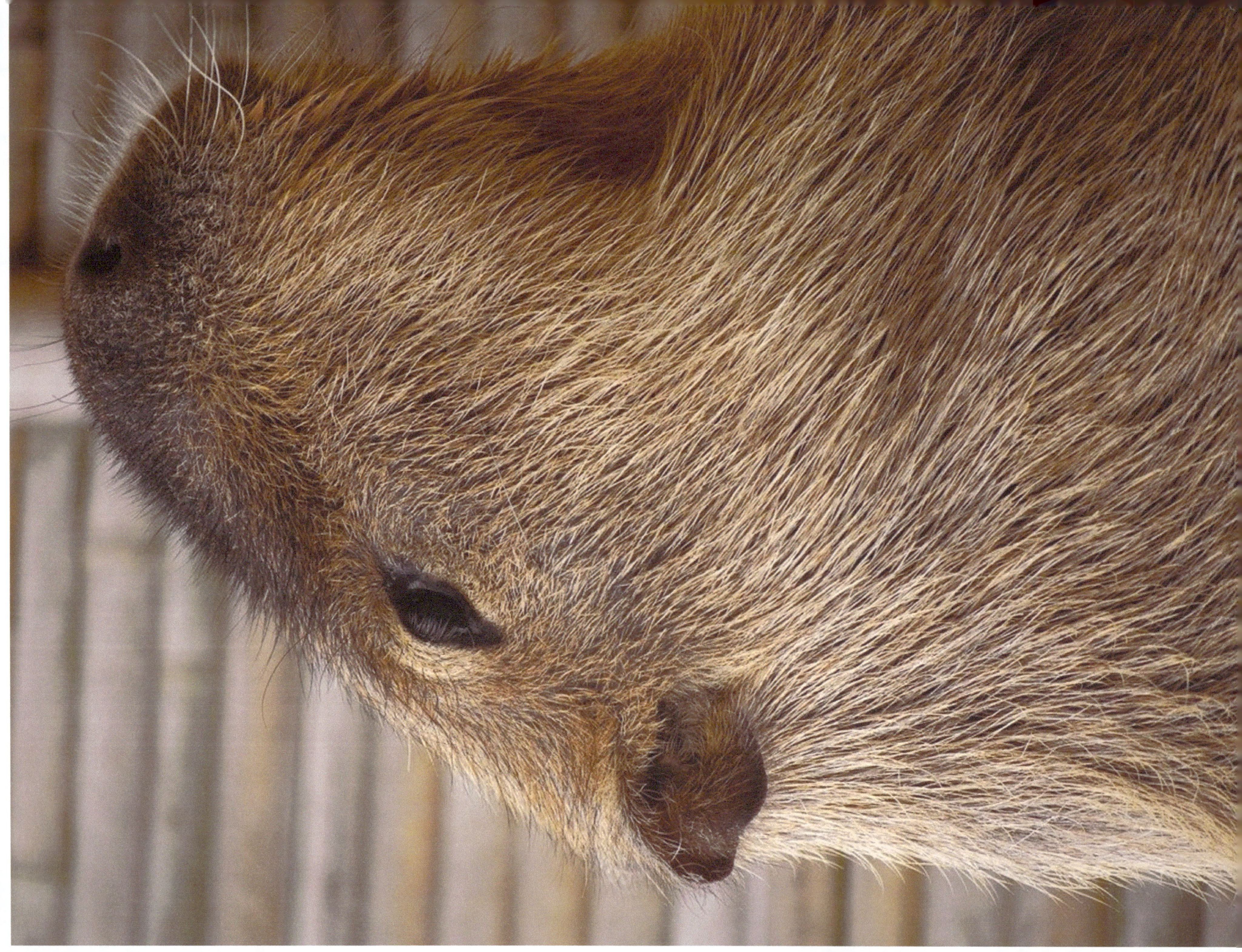

MARCH 2025

SUNDAY	MONDAY	TUESDAY	WEDNESDAY	THURSDAY	FRIDAY	SATURDAY
23	24	25	26	27	28	1
2	3	4	5	6	7	8
9	10	11	12	13	14	15
16	17	18	19	20	21	22
23 / 30	24 / 31	25	26	27	28	29

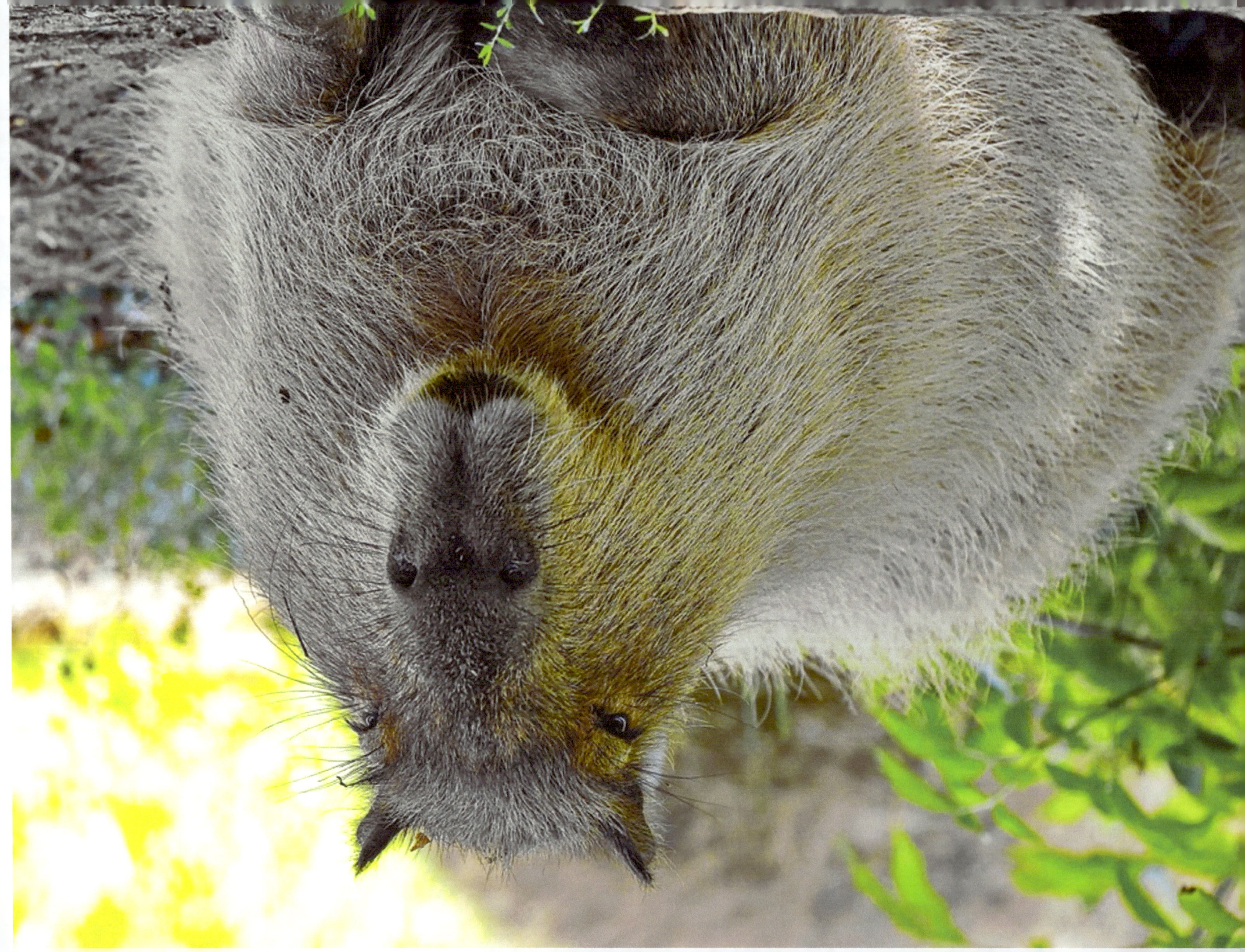

APRIL 2025

SUNDAY	MONDAY	TUESDAY	WEDNESDAY	THURSDAY	FRIDAY	SATURDAY
30	31	1	2	3	4	5
6	7	8	9	10	11	12
13	14	15	16	17	18	19
20	21	22	23	24	25	26
27	28	29	30	1	2	3

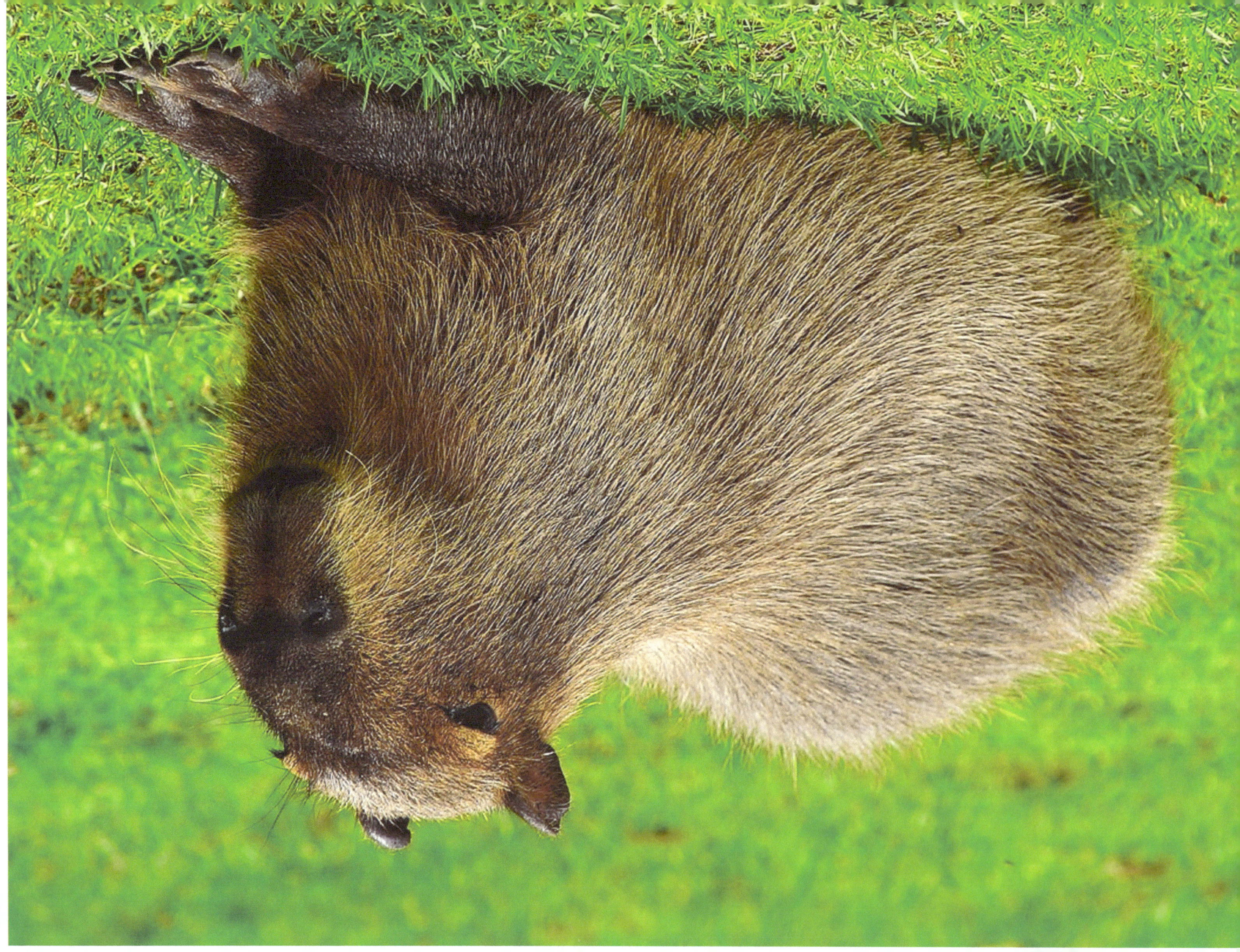

MAY 2025

SUNDAY	MONDAY	TUESDAY	WEDNESDAY	THURSDAY	FRIDAY	SATURDAY
27	28	29	30	1	2	3
4	5	6	7	8	9	10
11	12	13	14	15	16	17
18	19	20	21	22	23	24
25	26	27	28	29	30	31

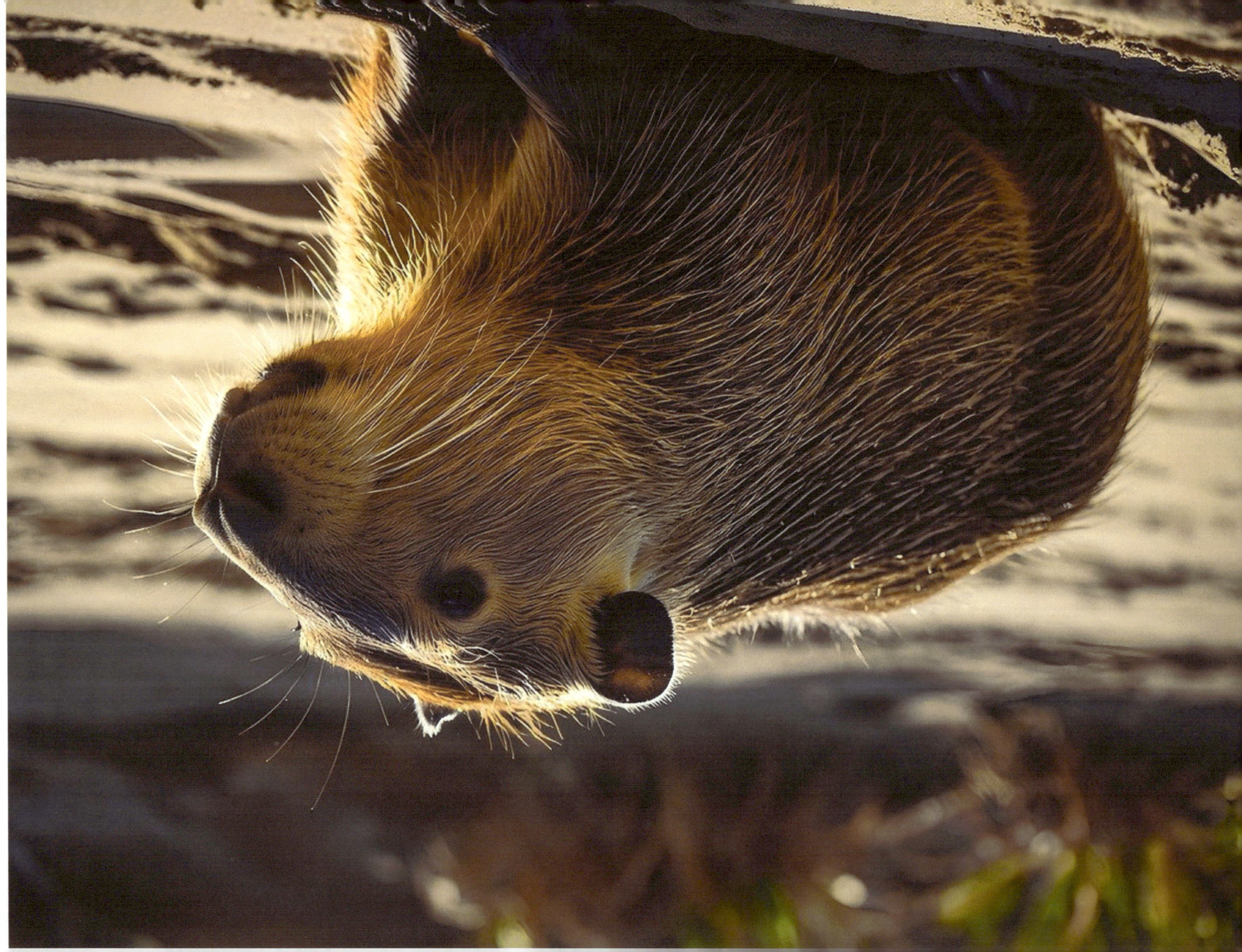

JUNE 2025

SUNDAY	MONDAY	TUESDAY	WEDNESDAY	THURSDAY	FRIDAY	SATURDAY
1	2	3	4	5	6	7
8	9	10	11	12	13	14
15	16	17	18	19	20	21
22	23	24	25	26	27	28
29	30	1	2	3	4	5

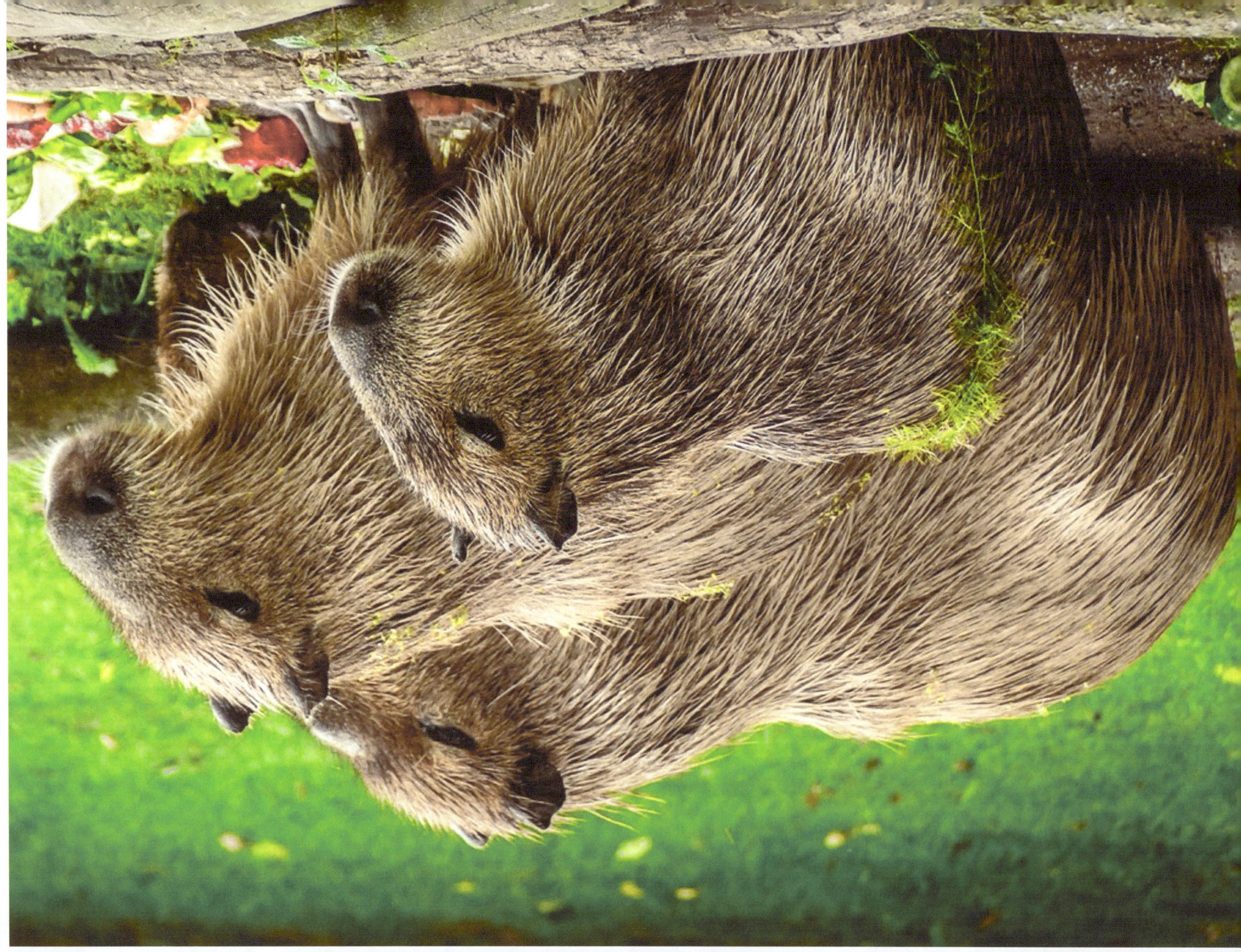

JULY 2025

SUNDAY	MONDAY	TUESDAY	WEDNESDAY	THURSDAY	FRIDAY	SATURDAY
29	30	1	2	3	4	5
6	7	8	9	10	11	12
13	14	15	16	17	18	19
20	21	22	23	24	25	26
27	28	29	30	31	1	2

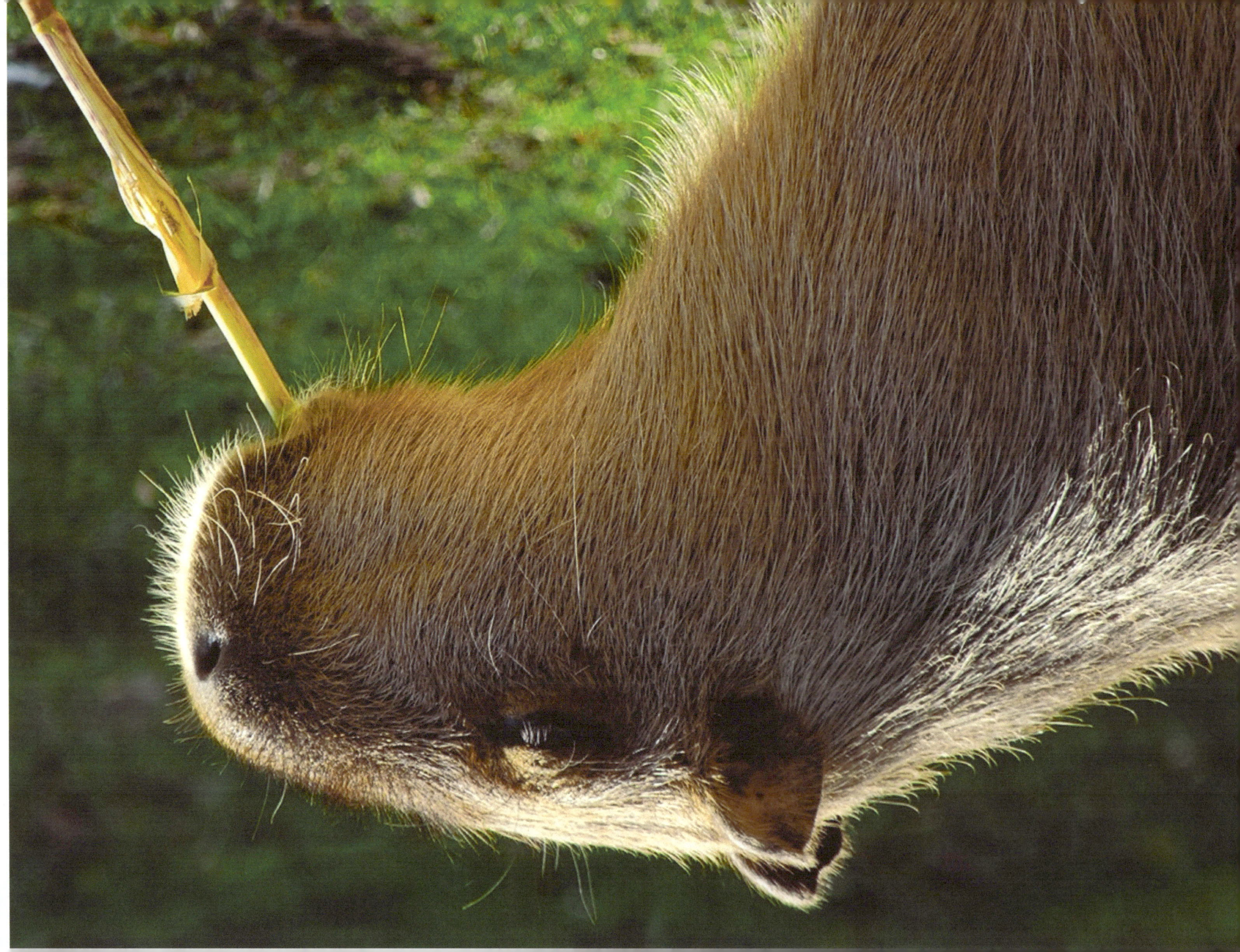

AUGUST 2025

SUNDAY	MONDAY	TUESDAY	WEDNESDAY	THURSDAY	FRIDAY	SATURDAY
27	28	29	30	31	1	2
3	4	5	6	7	8	9
10	11	12	13	14	15	16
17	18	19	20	21	22	23
24 / 31	25	26	27	28	29	30

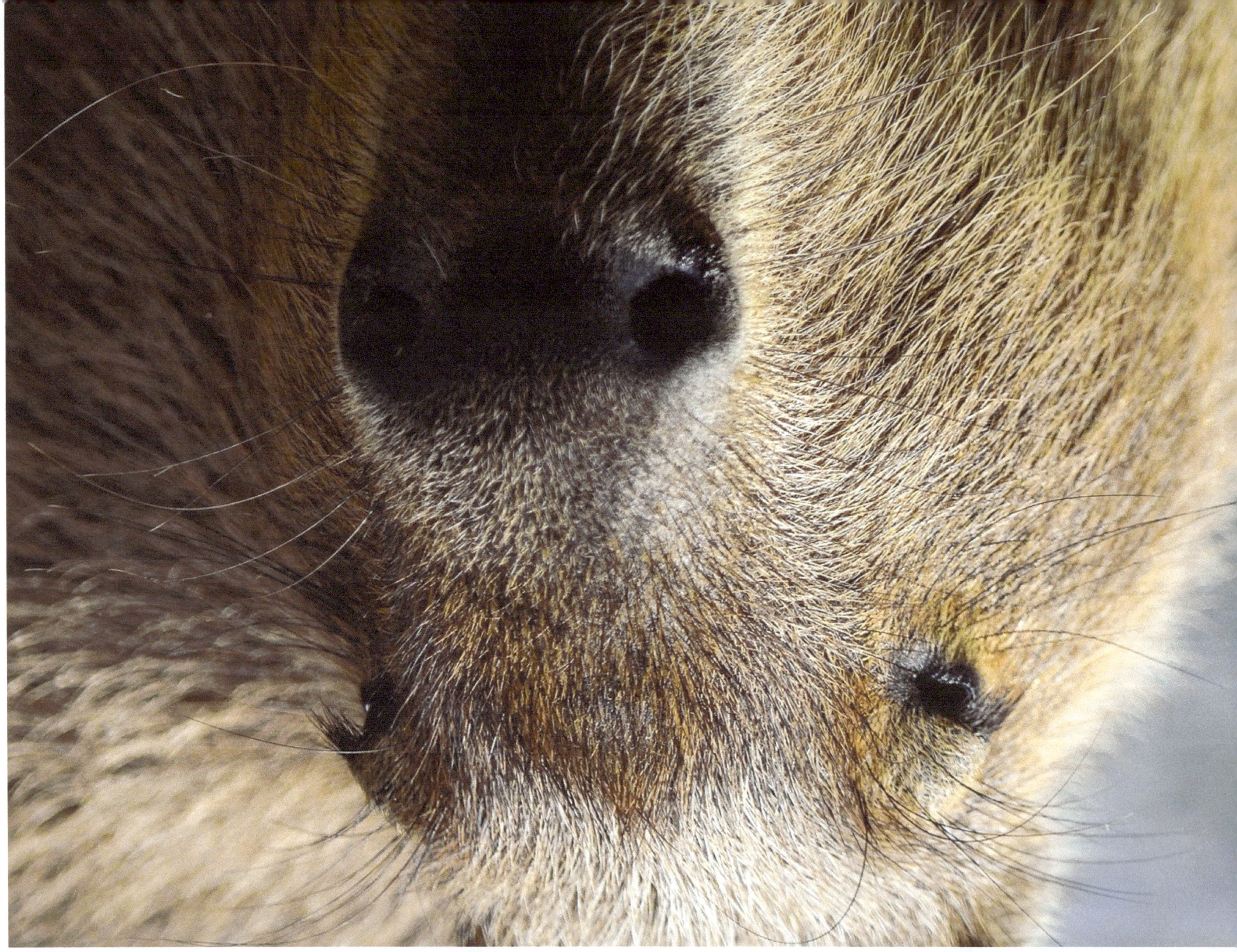

SEPTEMBER 2025

SUNDAY	MONDAY	TUESDAY	WEDNESDAY	THURSDAY	FRIDAY	SATURDAY
31	1	2	3	4	5	6
7	8	9	10	11	12	13
14	15	16	17	18	19	20
21	22	23	24	25	26	27
28	29	30	1	2	3	4

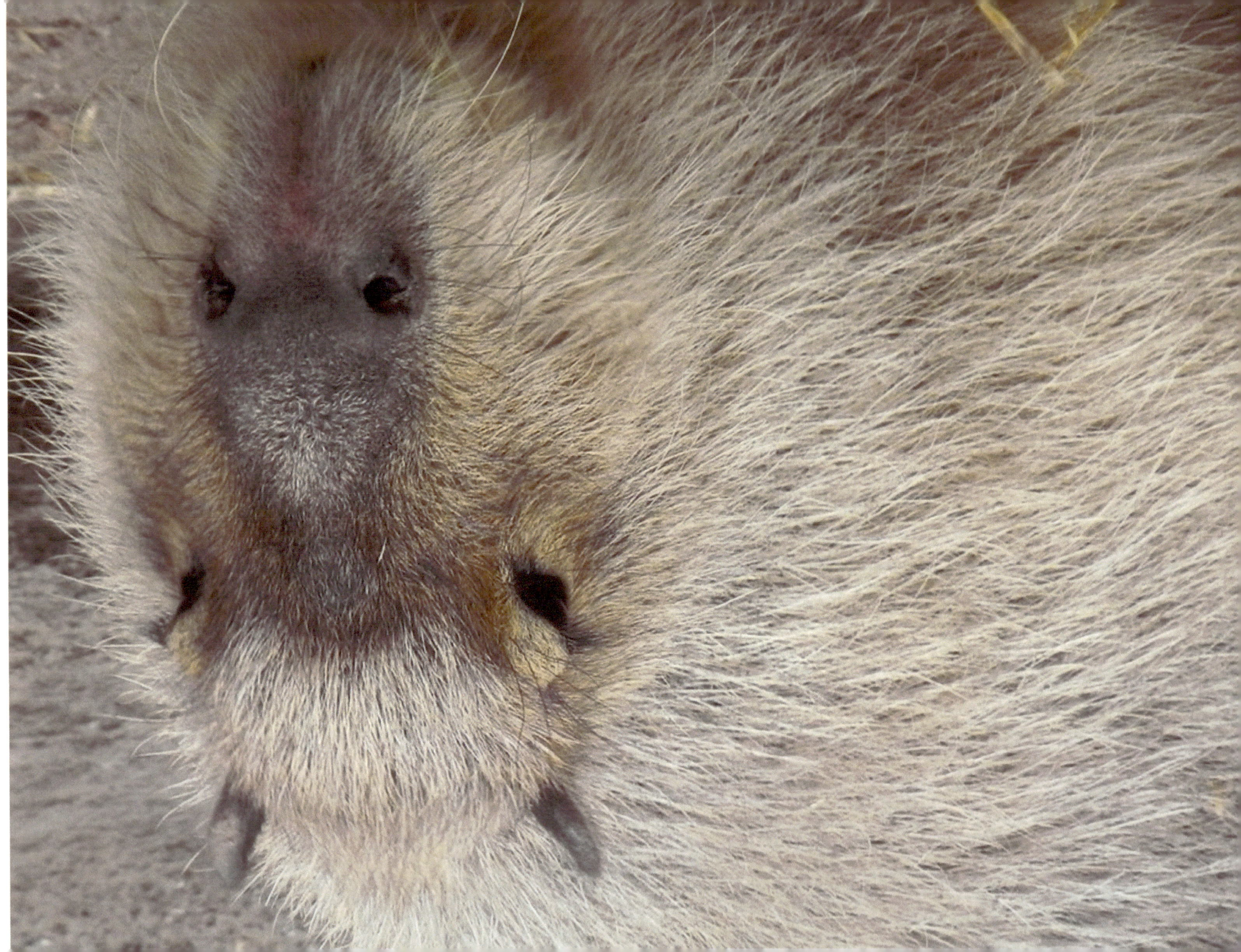

OCTOBER 2025

SUNDAY	MONDAY	TUESDAY	WEDNESDAY	THURSDAY	FRIDAY	SATURDAY
28	29	30	1	2	3	4
5	6	7	8	9	10	11
12	13	14	15	16	17	18
19	20	21	22	23	24	25
26	27	28	29	30	31	1

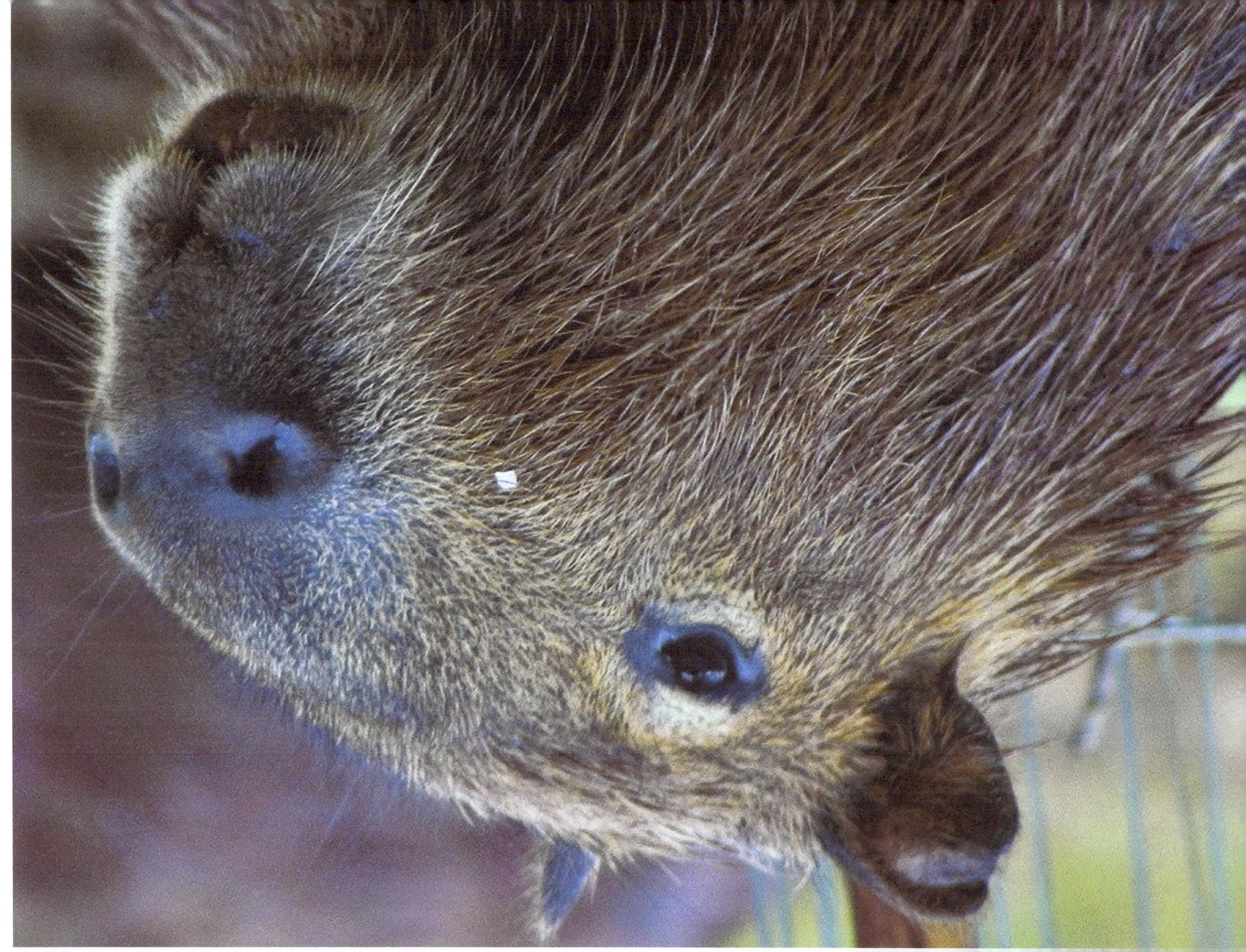

NOVEMBER 2025

SUNDAY	MONDAY	TUESDAY	WEDNESDAY	THURSDAY	FRIDAY	SATURDAY
26	27	28	29	30	31	1
2	3	4	5	6	7	8
9	10	11	12	13	14	15
16	17	18	19	20	21	22
23 / 30	24	25	26	27	28	29

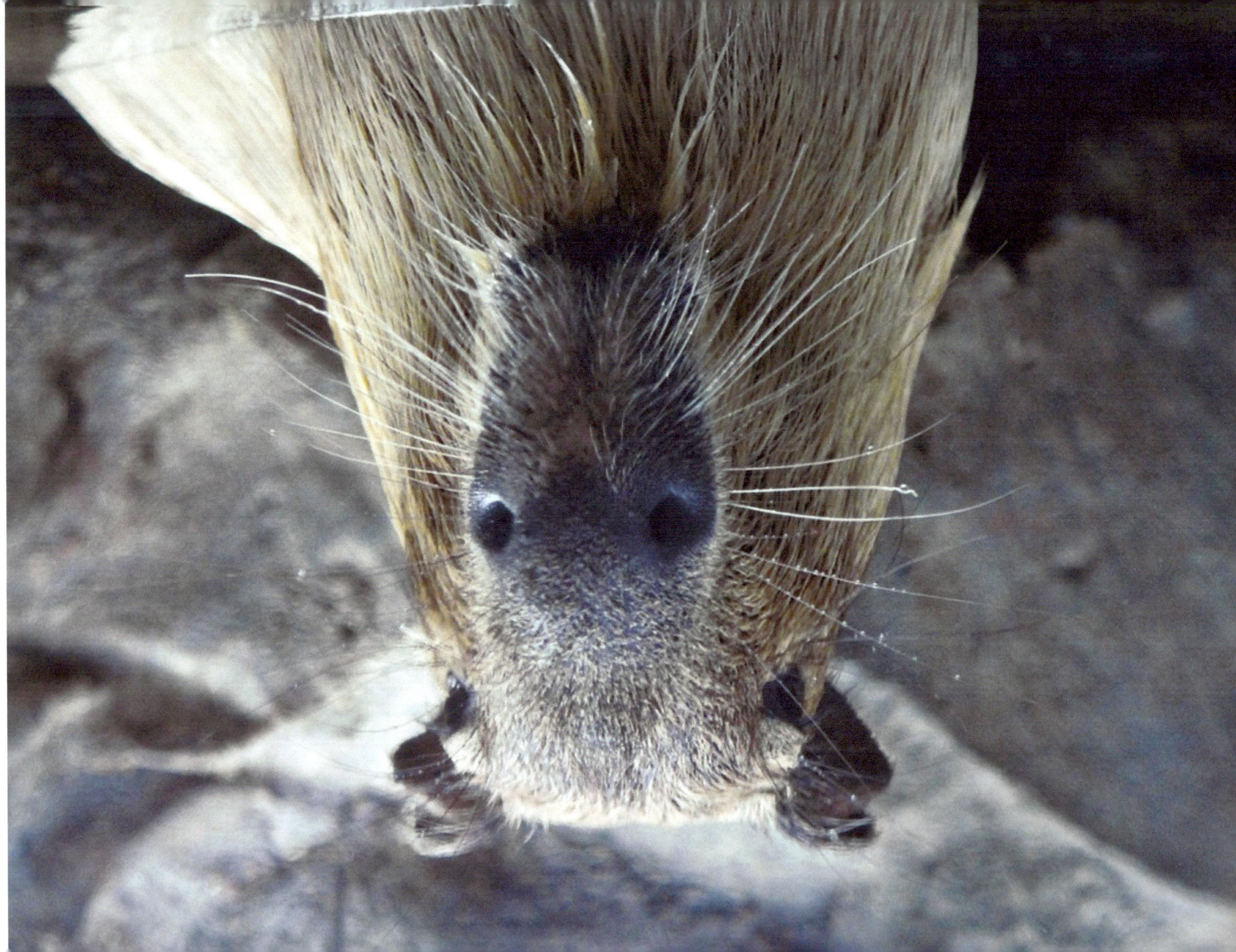

DECEMBER 2025

SUNDAY	MONDAY	TUESDAY	WEDNESDAY	THURSDAY	FRIDAY	SATURDAY
30	1	2	3	4	5	6
7	8	9	10	11	12	13
14	15	16	17	18	19	20
21	22	23	24	25	26	27
28	29	30	31	1	2	3

10 Facts About Capybaras

World's Largest Rodent: Capybaras hold the title as the world's largest rodent, with adults weighing between 77 and 150 pounds.

Excellent Swimmers: Capybaras are semi-aquatic animals with webbed feet, making them great swimmers who can stay underwater for up to five minutes to evade predators.

Social Creatures: Capybaras are very social animals that often live in groups of 10–20 but can form herds of up to 100 individuals during the dry season.

Vegetarian Diet: These gentle giants are herbivores, primarily munching on grasses, aquatic plants, and sometimes fruits or bark.

"Water Pigs": Their name comes from the native Guarani word kapi···va, meaning "master of the grasses," and they're often nicknamed "water pigs."

Eats Its Own Poop: Capybaras practice coprophagy (eating their own feces), which helps them re-digest food to absorb more nutrients.

Friend to Many Animals: They're known for their friendly and calm nature and are often seen with birds, monkeys, or even small mammals riding on their backs.

Adaptable Teeth: Capybaras' teeth keep growing throughout their lives, helping them continually chew on grasses and tougher plants without wearing down.

Scent Marking: Male capybaras have a scent gland on the top of their noses called a morillo, which they use to mark their territory.

Thermoregulation through Water: Capybaras use water not only to cool down but to regulate their body temperature, especially under the hot sun in their native habitats across South America.

Capybara Cafes Around The World

Capy B Cafe – Vancouver, Canada
Soon to open, this will be North America's first capybara cafe, offering cozy rooms for capybara interaction alongside a delightful menu of drinks and snacks

.Capybara Cafe – St. Augustine, Florida, USA
This cafe, run by Noah's Ark Sanctuary, combines capybara interaction with a mission to support wildlife, allowing guests to enjoy a close-up experience with capybaras

.Capybara Cafe – Milwaukee, Wisconsin, USA
Part of Crossroads Collective, this cafe specializes in Colombian street food inspired by Cali's traditions. Though it doesn't have live capybaras, it provides an authentic South American vibe

.Café Capyba – Tokyo, Japan
This popular spot in Tokyo allows guests to feed, pet, and take photos with capybaras. With a cozy environment, it's known for being one of Japan's best capybara cafes

iZoo – Shizuoka, Japan
Located near Tokyo, iZoo offers an outdoor capybara area for hands-on experiences. This zoo is a popular choice for those willing to

.
Hangzhou Capybara Cafe – Hangzhou, China
A trending spot in Hangzhou, this cafe provides a trendy ambiance combined with the joy of interacting with capybaras, attracting social media enthusiasts from across the region.

Capybara Land – Seoul, South Korea
Situated within a larger animal cafe, Capybara Land in Seoul allows guests to interact with capybaras along with other friendly animals, adding a memorable touch to any cafe visit.